WATERFOWL IDENTIFICATION

The LeMASTER METHOD

Richard LeMaster

0 11557 02982 6

STACKPOLE BOOKS

THE EASY WAY TO IDENTIFY WATERFOWL

Full instructions on page 7

Take all measurements of upper bill only –
from corner of mouth to tip

COLOR WILL VARY WITH AGE AND SEASON – USE CLOSEST SIZE AND SHAPE

Place thumbnail at corner of mouth and line
up with base line.

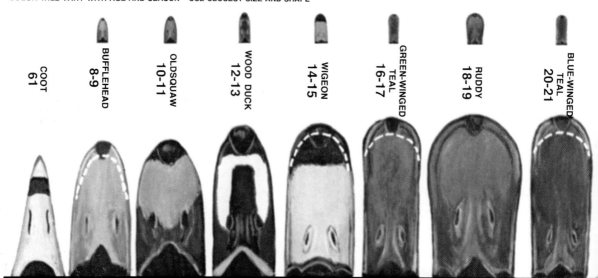

COOT
61

BUFFLEHEAD
8-9

OLDSQUAW
10-11

WOOD DUCK
12-13

WIGEON
14-15

GREEN-WINGED
TEAL
16-17

RUDDY
18-19

BLUE-WINGED
TEAL
20-21

Male bills shown full size. Female bill sizes are shown by dotted white lines, also in reduced form above for basic color only.

Place corner of mouth on base line.

Full instructions on page 75

COLOR WILL VARY WITH AGE AND SEASON – USE CLOSEST SIZE AND SHAPE

RING-NECKED
22-23

HOODED MERGANSER
24-25

LESSER SCAUP
26-27

COMMON
GOLDENEYE
28-29

CINNAMON TEAL
30-31

GREATER SCAUP
32-33

GADWALL
34-35

Male bills shown full size. Female bill sizes are shown by dotted white lines, also in reduced form above for basic color only.

Place corner of mouth on base line

Full instructions on page 75

COLOR WILL VARY WITH AGE AND SEASON – USE CLOSEST SIZE AND SHAPE

REDHEAD
36-37

BLACK SCOTER
38-39

PINTAIL
40-41

MALLARD
42-43

BLACK DUCK
44-45

SURF SCOTER
46-47

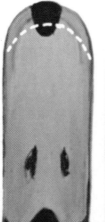

Male bills shown full size. Female bill sizes are shown by dotted white lines, also in reduced form above for basic color only.

Place corner of mouth on base line.

COLOR WILL VARY WITH AGE AND SEASON – USE CLOSEST SIZE AND SHAPE

Full instructions on page 75

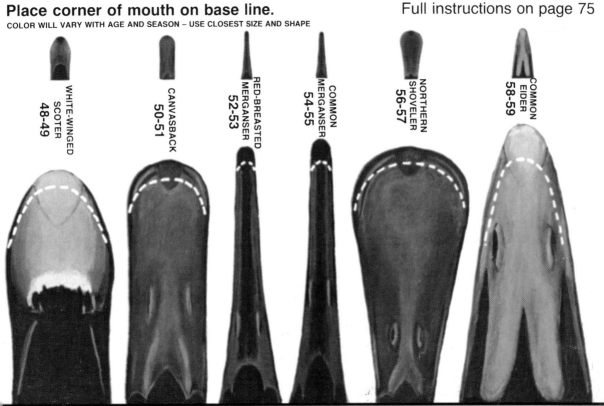

WHITE-WINGED SCOTER 48-49

CANVASBACK 50-51

RED-BREASTED MERGANSER 52-53

COMMON MERGANSER 54-55

NORTHERN SHOVELER 56-57

COMMON EIDER 58-59

Male bills shown full size. Female bill sizes are shown by dotted white lines, also in reduced form above for basic color only.

FOREWORD

Dick LeMaster's observations of the size and shape of duck bills provide an entirely new tool for recognizing species.

Dick is an unusually gifted person who has given up a lucrative business in industrial model building to further his first love, waterfowl. His talent and enthusiasm as a display decoy carver resulted in his first book *Wildlife in Wood*. His experience in preserving the living qualities of ducks in wood has given Dick a knowledge of form, feather arrangement, and color privy to few, if any, professionals. With his acute eye and photographic memory, he has observed differences between species that have heretofore been overlooked by professionals. In addition to his bill identification technique, Dick also focuses attention on another unique field identification concept, that of local altitudinal flight stratification. His renditions of heads, wings, and ducks in flight highlight specific differences that further aid identification. All in all, the contents of this booklet represent a significant breakthrough which will prove to be a blessing to the beginning waterfowler and veteran alike.

Frank C. Bellrose
Wildlife Specialist,
Illinois Natural History Survey

Author: *Ducks, Geese and Swans of North America*

The LeMaster Method of Waterfowl Identification

This guide introduces new aids for identifying waterfowl. One identifies the species of duck in hand; the other assists in determining the species in flight.

A duck in hand can be identified by the size and shape of its bill. Charts are provided for the user to match a bill in hand with the outlines of the particular species. The full size and shape of the bill is repeated on the pages for each species, along with information to solidify the selection. Juveniles of both sexes have bills that are slightly smaller, but even these will fall within the basic size and shape of the species. Color of the bill is of lesser importance because it will vary with age and season.

Although positive identification is provided through this method, it should be understood that every effort should be made to identify a duck before you have it in hand.

To aid in-flight identification, this method introduces a new dimension – Levels (strata or layer) of flight that the various species fly in over open water, and these are divided into four distinct levels. The study and use of this dimension, coupled with flock characteristics and species markings, will aid your in-flight identification.

Through artwork, I have shown only what you should focus your attention on. In flight; the relative shades formed are more apparent than distinctive color and definition.

For identifying birds in hand, I have shown only heads and the area on the wing that is of the greatest importance – all other detail is omitted to avoid confusion.

Good luck, and may our paths cross many times.

Artwork by author

BUFFLEHEAD
Bucephala albeola

MALE
Length 15"

Juvenile

In-flight: Level 1 – Low to the water, direct line, small flocks.

Comparisons: pages 70-71.

In hand:

Adult: White patch on dark multi-color head, white wing patch.

Juvenile male: Small white patch starts at edge of eye – behind and below on female. Grayish rump feathers and traces of pink on gray feet.

FEMALE
Length 13"

BUFFLEHEAD
Bucephala albeola

In-flight: Level 1 – Low to the water, direct line, small flocks.

Comparisons: pages 72-73.

In hand:

Female: Very small, dark brown head with white patch behind and below eye. Check wing markings; juvenile male is similar to female. The larger bill of the male usually separates the sexes.

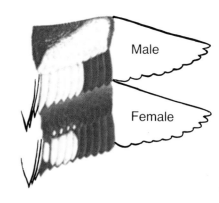

Male

Female

9

OLDSQUAW
Clangula hyemalis

MALE
Length 20''

In-flight: Level 1 – Low to the water, twisting and turning, small flocks.

Comparisons: pages 70-71.

In hand:

Adult male: Pinkish saddle over end of bill with black tip, elongated tail. Dark breast of male separates sexes in both winter and summer plumage.

FEMALE
Length 15"

OLDSQUAW
Clangula hyemalis

In-flight: Level 1 – Low to the water, twisting and turning, small flocks.

Comparisons: page 72-73

In hand:

Female: Identified by bill, chunky white body and dark back. Dark underwing separates from other species.

11

WOOD DUCK
Aix sponsa

MALE
Length 20''

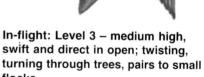

In-flight: Level 3 – medium high, swift and direct in open; twisting, turning through trees, pairs to small flocks.

Comparisons: pages 70-71

In hand:

Adult male: Vividly colored bill, multi-iridescent head with white markings. Blue and silver color on wing tip also separates from other species.

FEMALE
Length 19''

WOOD DUCK
Aix sponsa

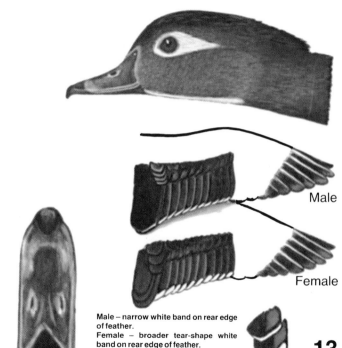

In-flight: Level 3 – medium high, swift and direct in open; twisting, turning through trees, pairs to small flocks.

Comparisons: pages 72-73

In hand:

Female: Easily distinguished by white tear-drop shape around eye. Also tear-drop shape white on rear inner edge of wing.

Male

Female

Male – narrow white band on rear edge of feather.
Female – broader tear-shape white band on rear edge of feather.

13

WIGEON
Anas americana

MALE
Length 20"

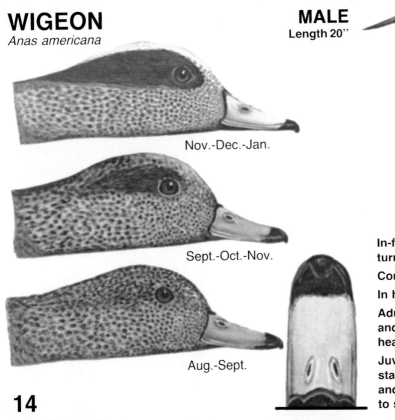

Nov.-Dec.-Jan.

Sept.-Oct.-Nov.

Aug.-Sept.

In-flight: Level 4 – high, twisting, turning, bunched flock.

Comparisons: pages 70-71

In hand:

Adult male: Distinctive light crown and iridescent green patch on head.

Juvenile male: Hen-like, but has start of rosy-gray feathers at neckline and vermiculated feathers beginning to show (page 74).

14

FEMALE
Length 19"

WIGEON
Anas americana

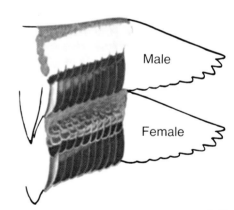

Male

Female

In-flight: Level 4 – high, twisting, turning, bunched flock.

Comparisons: page 72-73

In hand:

Female: Separated from other species by size, shape, and color of bill; also wing markings.

15

GREEN-WINGED TEAL

Anas crecca carolinensis

MALE
Length 15"

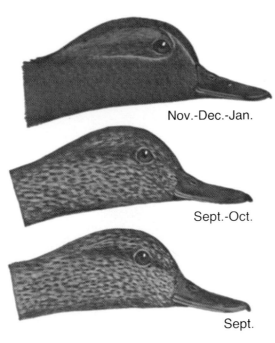

Nov.-Dec.-Jan.

Sept.-Oct.

Sept.

In-fight: Level 3 – medium high, erratic, compact flocks. (lower over marshy area).

Comparisons: pages 70-71

In hand:

Adult male: Chestnut red head with iridescent green mask and vivid green patch on wing are Green-wing characteristics.

Juvenile male: Similar in appearance to female, but has vermiculated feathers starting in on rump and side area (page 74). Reddish feathers may show on head.

16

FEMALE GREEN-WINGED TEAL
Length 14"

Anas crecca carolinensis

In-flight: Level 3 – medium high, erratic, compact flocks. (lower over marshy area).

Comparisons: pages 72-73

In hand:

Female: Bill is smaller, lighter colored than male; usually spotted. Vivid green patch on wing separates from all other females.

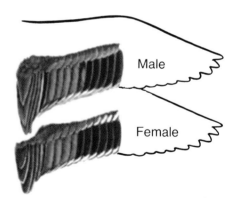

Male

Female

17

RUDDY DUCK
Oxyura jamaicensis rubida

MALE
Length 15"

Summer plumage

Winter plumage

In-flight: Level 1 – Low to the water, small flocks.

Comparisons: pages 71-72

In hand:

Male: Brightly colored during summer only. Fall and winter, male is dark, mottled sometimes with rust colored feathers. Light patch on head is not as white as in summer.

18

FEMALE
Length 15"

RUDDY DUCK
Oxyura jamaicensis rubida

In-flight: Level 1 – low to the water, small flocks.

Comparisons: pages 72-73

In hand:

Female: Bill size and shape separates from other species. Light patch on head has darker feathers through center simulating stripe.

Wing – Both Sexes

19

BLUE-WINGED TEAL
Anas discors

MALE
Length 16"

spring

fall and winter

Sept.-Dec.

Dec.-Jan.

Jan.-Feb.

In flight: Level 3 – medium high, twisting, turning, compact flocks. (lower over marshy area).

Comparisons: pages 70-71

In hand:

Male: Looks like female early fall to winter. Bill and patch on wing separates from all species except Cinnamon Teal. Bill size is larger on the Cinnamon. White line of feathers on wing separates sex easily – female is mottled.

20

FEMALE
Length 14''

BLUE-WINGED TEAL
Anas discors

In flight: Level 3 – medium high,
twisting, turning, compact flocks.
(lower over marshy area).

In hand:

Female: Identified by bill size and
shape, blue patch and mottled
feathers on the wing.

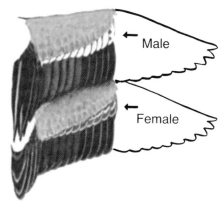

Male

Female

RING-NECKED
Aythya collaris

Juvenile

In flight: Level 2 – medium low, open formation, small flocks. (frequents ponds and marshes).

Comparisons: pages 70-71

In hand:

Adult male: Has two white rings on bill. Knob on back of head and dark back also separates from Scaup. Brown ring on neck shows in good light.

Juvenile male: Has darker breast than female and eye may be more yellowish. Vermiculated feathers may show (page 74).

22

RING-NECKED
Aythya collaris

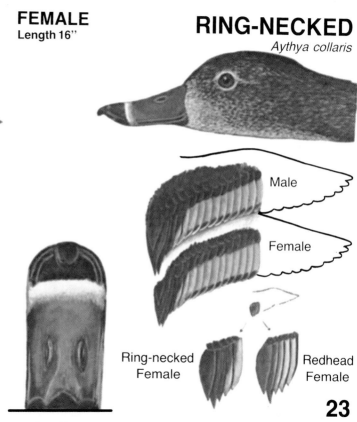

Male

Female

Ring-necked
Female

Redhead
Female

In-flight: Level 2 – medium low, open formation, small flocks. (frequents ponds and marshes)

Comparisons: pages 72-73

In hand:

Female: Best identified by bill, size and shape, wing, and light ring around eye. Head has more salt and pepper gray than similar Redhead female. Bill and wing separates from Redhead also.

23

HOODED MERGANSER

Mergus cucullatus

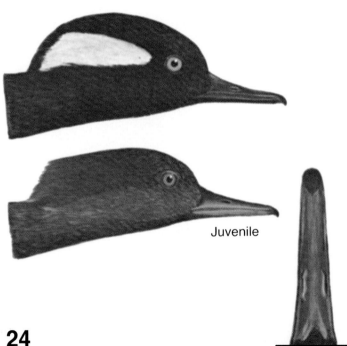

Juvenile

In-flight: Level 1 – low to the water, direct, pairs to small flocks.

Comparisons: pages 70-71

In hand:

Adult male: Readily identified by bill and black head with white patch, tipped with black. Full plumage at 2½ years.

Juvenile male: Similar in appearance to female but eye has more yellow in it.

FEMALE
Length 17"

HOODED MERGANSER
Mergus cucullatus

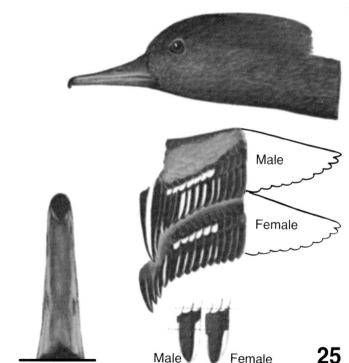

Male

Female

Male   Female

In-flight: Level 1 – low to the water, direct, pairs to small flocks.

Comparisons: pages 72-73

In hand:

Female: Bill identifies species. Wing is key for sexing adults only.

25

LESSER SCAUP
Aythya affinis

MALE
Length 17"

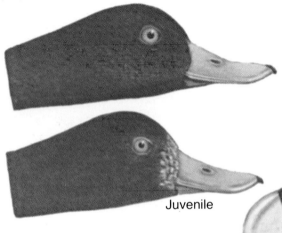

Juvenile

Juvenile male: Purple feathers starting on head, yellowish eye and vermiculated feathers emerging (page 74).

In-flight: Level 2 – medium low, erratic, close bunched flocks.

Comparisons: pages 70-71

In hand:

Adult male: Commonly called "Bluebill". Bill size, shape, and color separates from other species. Vermiculated back and body identifies sex as male (page 74). Wing markings will separate from Greater Scaup which is similar.

LESSER SCAUP
Aythya affinis

Lesser Scaup
(both sexes)

Greater Scaup
(both sexes)

In-flight: Level 2 – medium low, erratic, close bunched flocks.

Comparisons: pages 72-73

In hand:

Female: Identified by the bill and white mask on head. The wing markings will separate from the similar Greater Scaup female.

27

COMMON GOLDENEYE
Bucephala clangula americana

MALE
Length 19''

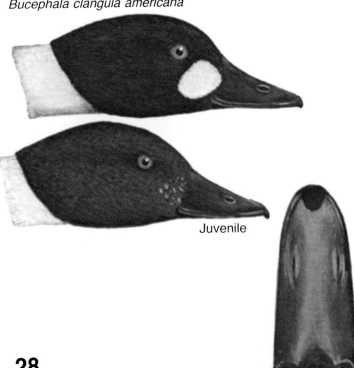

Juvenile

In-flight: Level 2 – medium low, small flocks. Wings make whistling sound.

Comparisons: pages 70-71

In hand:

Adult male: Identified by bill size and shape and white circle patch between eye and bill.

Juvenile male: Similar to female but does not have orangish patch on bill. Bill is larger than female. Full adult plumage at 2½ years.

28

FEMALE
Length 17"

COMMON GOLDENEYE
Bucephala clangula americana

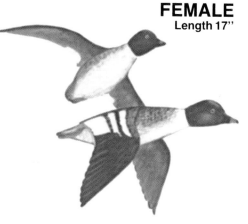

In-flight: Level 2 – medium low, small flocks. Wings make whistling sound.

Comparisons: pages 72-73

In hand:

Female: Identified by bill shape and color, dark brown head and grayish body. Wing is solid indicator.

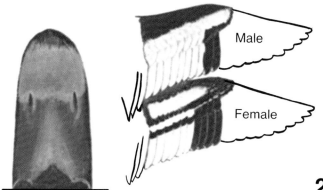

Male

Female

29

CINNAMON TEAL

Anas cyanoptera septentrionalium

MALE
Length 16"

both plumages

Jan.-Feb.

Sept.-Dec.

In-flight: Level 3 — medium high, twisting, turning, compact flocks. (lower over marshy area).

Comparisons: pages 70-71

In hand:

Adult male: Bill size and shape separates species. Wing markings are identical to Blue-winged Teal. Cinnamon color of male is spring plumage; fall and winter is similar in appearance to female.

Juvenile male: Length of bill and white feathers on wing will separate it from female.

FEMALE
Length 15"

CINNAMON TEAL
Anas cyanoptera septentrionalium

In-flight: Level 3 – medium high, twisting, turning, compact flocks. (lower over marshy area).

Comparisons: pages 72-73

In hand:

Female: Identified by bill size and wing. Very similar to Blue-winged Teal female but bill is longer and narrows at head. Sides of bill are parallel on Blue-winged Teal female when viewed from the top.

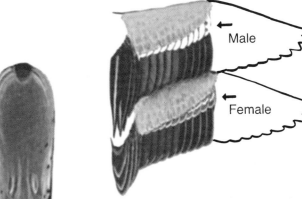

Male

Female

31

GREATER SCAUP
Aythya marila mariloides

MALE
Length 18"

In-flight: level 2 – medium low, erratic, close bunched flocks.

Comparisons: pages 70-71

In hand:

Adult male: Identified by bill size, shape, and color. Extended wing markings separate species from the similar Lesser Scaup male.

FEMALE
Length 17"

GREATER SCAUP
Aythya marila mariloides

In-flight: Level 2 – medium low, erratic, close bunched flocks.

Comparisons: pages 72-73

In hand:

Female: Identical to Lesser Scaup female except for being larger. The size, shape, and color of the bill will separate from all other species. Extended wing markings will separate from the similar Lesser Scaup female.

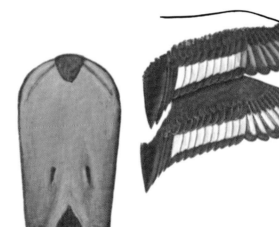

Lesser Scaup
(both sexes)

Greater Scaup
(both sexes)

33

GADWALL
Anas strepera

Juvenile

In-flight: level 4 – high, direct, compact flocks.

Comparisons: pages 70-71

In hand:

Adult male: Identified by bill, size and shape, also wing markings.

Juvenile male: Similar in appearance to female but usually lacks spots on orangish bill. Vermiculated feathers may be starting to show (page 74).

FEMALE
Length 19"

GADWALL
Anas strepera

In-flight: Level 4 – high, direct, compact flocks.

Comparisons: pages 72-73

In hand:

Female: Bill size, shape, and color, will identify from other females. Wing markings will separate from the similar Mallard female.

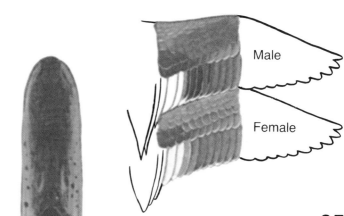

Male

Female

35

REDHEAD
Aythya americana

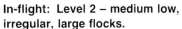

Dec.-Jan.

Oct.-Dec.

In-flight: Level 2 – medium low, irregular, large flocks.

Comparisons: pages 70-71

In hand:

Adult male: Distinguished by bill shape and color, reddish head, and yellow eye.

Juvenile male: Has brownish head, darker bill, yellowish eye and vermiculated feathers (page 74).

FEMALE
Length 19''

REDHEAD
Aythya americana

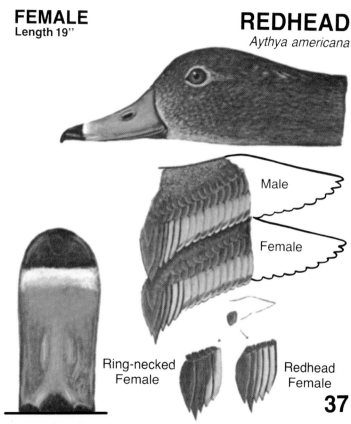

Male

Female

Ring-necked Female

Redhead Female

In-flight: Level 2 – medium low, irregular, large flocks.

Comparisons: pages 72-73

In hand:

Female: Most accurately identified by bill size and shape, and wing markings. Redhead female has more gray feathers with black edges (rear inner wing) than similar Ring-necked female.

37

BLACK SCOTER
Melanitta nigra americana

MALE
Length 20''

Black
White-winged
Surf

Male scoters
Differences in bill shapes and eye colors.

38

In-flight: Level 1 – low to the water, small flocks.

Comparisons: pages 70-71

In hand:

Adult male: Bill size and shape will separate from other species. Dark feet separate it from other Scoters.

Juvenile male: Similar to female but is larger and has lighter breast.

FEMALE
Length 19"

BLACK SCOTER
Melanitta nigra americana

Both sexes have dark wings with no definite markings.

Black

White-winged

Surf

Female and Juvenile Scoters Difference in bill shapes.

In-flight: Level 2 – low to the water, small flocks.

Comparisons: pages 72-73

In hand:

Female: Best identified by bill shape and dark feet. Bill is best indicator for identification of Scoters.

39

PINTAIL
Anas acuta acuta

Length 25"

Dec.-Jan.

Oct.-Nov.-Dec.

Sept.-Oct.

In-flight: Level 4 – high, graceful fliers.

Comparisons: pages 70-71

In hand:

Adult male: Identified by bill shape and color. The wing markings, long tail, and white hook on back of head are positive indicators.

Juvenile male: Similar to female but bill is larger and vermiculation may start showing on sides (page 74).

40

FEMALE
Length 21"

PINTAIL
Anas acuta acuta

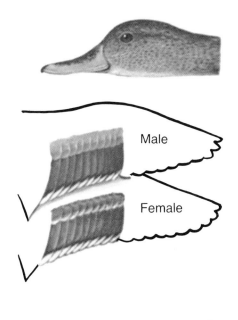

Male

Female

In-flight: Level 4 – high, graceful fliers.

Comparisons: pages 72-73

In hand:

Female: Identified by bill size and shape and wing markings.

41

MALLARD
Anas platyrhynchos platyrhynchos

MALE
Length 25''

Nov.-Dec.-Jan.

Sept.-Oct.

Aug.-Sept.

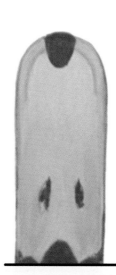

In-flight: Level 4 – high, direct, steady, large flocks.

Comparisons: pages 70-71

In hand:

Adult male: Identified by bill, wing markings, bright green iridescent head, and white neck ring.

Juvenile male: Similar in appearance to female but will have greenish bill, not orange as on female. Vermiculated feathers may show in areas (page 74).

42

FEMALE
Length 23''

MALLARD
Anas platyrhynchos platyrhynchos

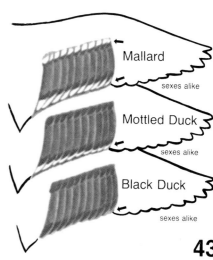

Mallard

sexes alike

Mottled Duck

sexes alike

Black Duck

sexes alike

In-flight: Level 4 – high, direct, steady, large flocks.

Comparisons: pages 72-73

In hand:

Female: Identified by size, shape, and color of bill, and wing markings.

43

BLACK DUCK
Anas rubripes

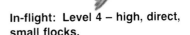

In-flight: Level 4 – high, direct, small flocks.

Comparisons: pages 70-71

In hand:

Adult male: Identified by bill size and shape, wing markings, and dark body with no vermiculation (page 74). Bill can vary in color from light olive green to yellow.

Juvenile: Separated from female by bill size and lack of dark color on ridge of bill.

FEMALE
Length 21''

BLACK DUCK
Anas rubripes

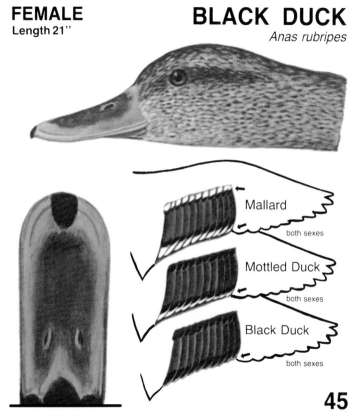

Mallard
both sexes

Mottled Duck
both sexes

Black Duck
both sexes

In-flight: Level 4 – high, direct, small flocks.

Comparisons: pages 72-73

In hand:

Female: Wing markings will identify species, olive green bill with dark saddle on ridge is female exclusive.

Mottled Duck: Wing markings are most positive identification, body is darker than Mallard female, browner than Black Duck female.

45

SURF SCOTER
Melanitta perspicillata

MALE
Length 20''

Black

White-winged

Surf

Male Scoters: Differences in bill shapes and eye colors.

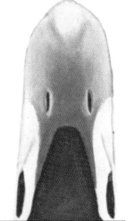

In-flight: Level 1 – low to the water, irregular large flocks.

Comparisons: pages 70-71

In hand:

Adult male: Identified by coloration, shape and size of bill, and the white markings on the black head. Attains full color at 2½ years.

Juvenile male: Similar to female but patches on head are whiter.

FEMALE
Length 18"

SURF SCOTER
Melanitta perspicillata

Wings are dark
No specific markings

Black
White-winged
Surf

Female and Juvenile Scoters:
Difference in bill shapes.

In-flight: Level 1 – low to the water, irregular large flocks.

Comparisons: pages 72-73

In hand:

Female: Identified by the size, shape of the bill,and the dark patch near base of bill.

47

WHITE-WINGED SCOTER
Melanitta fusca deglandi

MALE
Length 22"

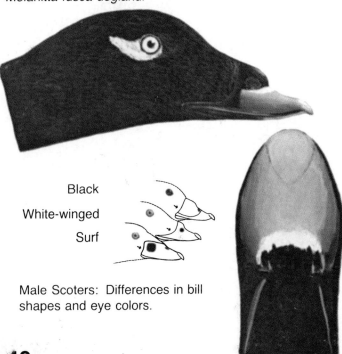

Black

White-winged

Surf

Male Scoters: Differences in bill shapes and eye colors.

In-flight: Level 1 – low to the water, long lines or loose flocks.

Comparisons: pages 70-71

In hand:

Adult male: Identified by bill, wing markings, and white around eye.

Juvenile male: Similar to female but has grayish eye; female has brown eye.

48

FEMALE
Length 21"

WHITE-WINGED SCOTER

Melanitta fusca deglandi

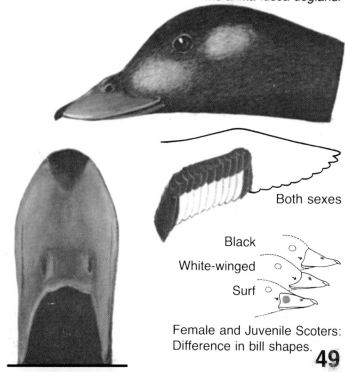

Both sexes

Black
White-winged
Surf

Female and Juvenile Scoters:
Difference in bill shapes.

In-flight: Level 1 – low to the water, long lines or loose flocks.

Comparisons: pages 72-73

In hand:

Female: Identified by bill size and shape, and the wing markings. Eye is brown; juvenile male is grayish.

49

CANVASBACK

Aythya valisineria

MALE
Length 21"

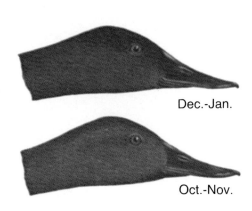

Dec.-Jan.

Oct.-Nov.

In-flight: Level 2 – medium low, normally irregular but sometimes V or linelike, small flocks.

Comparisons: pages 70-71

In hand:

Adult male: Identified by bill shape and size, eye color, and wing markings.

Juvenile male: Bill size and shape will separate from other species. May show start of vermiculated feathers (page 74).

FEMALE
Length 20''

CANVASBACK
Aythya valisineria

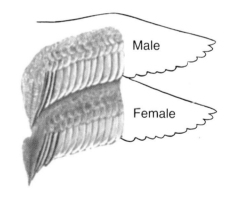

Male

Female

In-flight: Level 2 – medium low,
normally irregular but sometimes V
or linelike, small flocks.

Comparisons: pages 72-73

In hand:

Female: Identified by size and shape
of bill and wing markings. Bill will
definitely separate it from other
similar females.

51

RED-BREASTED MERGANSER

Mergus serrator

MALE
Length 17"

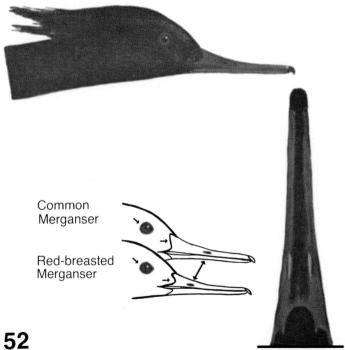

Common
Merganser

Red-breasted
Merganser

In-flight: Level 1 – low to the water, line formation, small flocks.

Comparisons: pages 70-71

In hand:

Adult male: Bill size and shape, separates from all others except Common Merganser. Location of nostrils, green head with tufts on back, red eye, and vermiculated feathers (page 74) will separate from the Common Merganser male.

Juvenile male: Will have blackish feathers on head starting in December, also may start showing some vermiculation (page 74).

52

RED-BREASTED MERGANSER

Mergus serrator

In-flight: Level 1 – low to the water, line formation, small flocks.

Comparisons: pages 72-73

In hand:

Female: Bill size and shape, separates from all others except Common Merganser. Location of nostril, reddish eye, and the lack of definite whitish throat will separate from the similar Common Merganser female.

Common
Merganser

Red-breasted
Merganser

53

COMMON MERGANSER

Mergus merganser americanus

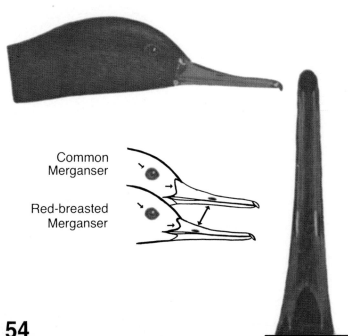

Common
Merganser

Red-breasted
Merganser

In-flight: Level 1 – low to the water, line formation, small flocks.

Comparisons: pages 70-71

In hand:

Adult male: Bill will separate from all other species except the Red-breasted Merganser. Nostrils near center of bill, lack of tufts on back of head, and brown eye are Common Merganser male features. Body is pinkish white.

54

FEMALE
Length 23"

COMMON MERGANSER
Mergus merganser americanus

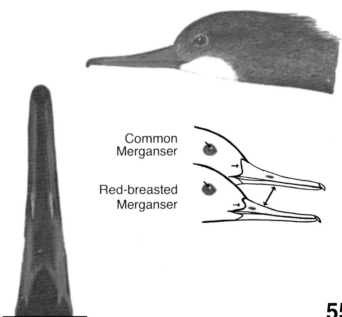

Common Merganser

Red-breasted Merganser

In-flight: Level 1 – low to the water, line formation, small flocks.

Comparisons: pages 72-73

In hand:

Female: Separated by bill shape and size from all species except Red-breasted Merganser. The Common Merganser female has nostril near center of bill, darker eye, definite whitish throat, and is larger than Red-breasted female.

55

NORTHERN SHOVELER

Anas clypeata

Jan.-Feb.

Nov.-Dec.

Sept.-Oct.

In-flight: Level 3 – medium high, erratic, small flocks.

Comparisons: pages 70-71

In hand:

Adult male: Easily identified by the shape and size of the bill. Will have black bill, yellow eye, and vivid body colors in late winter.

Juvenile and early plumage: Resembles female but bill is larger, usually lacking the dark spots, eye more yellowish, and blue patch on wing is brighter than female. Check wing difference also.

56

NORTHERN SHOVELER

Anas clypeata

FEMALE
Length 19"

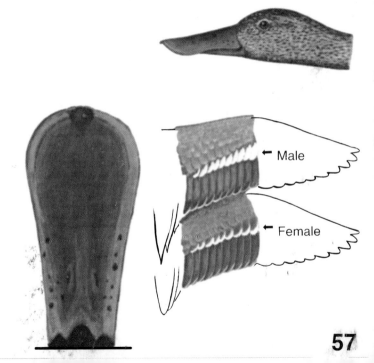

← Male

← Female

In-flight: Level 3 – medium high, erratic, small flocks.

Comparisons: pages 72-73

In hand:

Female: Identified by shape and size of bill and wing markings.

COMMON EIDER
Somateria mollissima

MALE
Length 24"

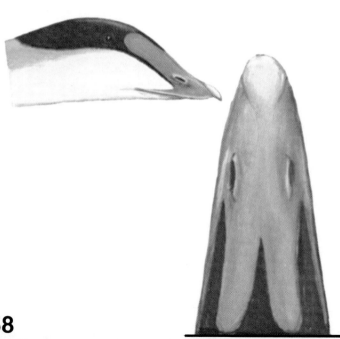

In-flight: Level 1 – low to the water, slow and sluggish.

Comparisons: pages 70-71

In hand:

Adult male: Distinguished from other Eider males by the black mask and the shape of the bill. Pacific Eider is similar but has orangish bill. All species of Eider males have some light yellow green on head.

FEMALE
Length 23"

COMMON EIDER
Somateria mellissima

In-flight: Level 1 – low to the water, slow and sluggish.

Comparisons: pages 72-73

In hand:

Female: Identified by the shape and size of the bill. Bill shapes are different on females of other Eider species.

59

BARROW'S GOLDENEYE

Bucephala islandica

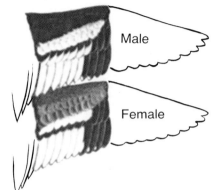

Male

Female

MALE
Length 19''

FEMALE
Length 17''

Female

Male

In-flight: Level 2 – medium low, small flocks.

In hand:

Adult male: Identified by bill size, shape and white crescent on head.

Female: Separated from the similar Common Goldeneye female by the size and shape of the bill and wing markings.

AMERICAN COOT
Fulica americana

Length 15"
Sexes alike

In-flight: Level 1 – low to the water

Comparisons: pages 72-73

In hand:

Male and female: Sexes similar. Identified by bill, feet, white under tail, and on trailing edge of wing.

61

HARLEQUIN DUCK
Histrionicus histrionicus

MALE
Length 17''

FEMALE
Length 16''

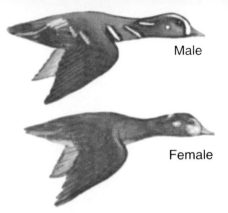

Male

Female

In-flight: Level 1 – low to the water, small flocks.

In hand:

Adult male: Identified easily by vividly contrasting, colors of head and body.

Female: Similar to Bufflehead female but is larger and has three light patches on the head instead of one. Oldsquaw female is lighter in color and the female Surf Scoter is larger.

WHISTLING DUCKS

FULVOUS WHISTLING DUCK
Dendrocygna bicolor helva

Length 18"

Gray bill and feet separates from other Whistling Ducks.

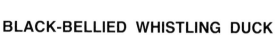

BLACK-BELLIED WHISTLING DUCK
Dendrocygna autumnalis autumnalis

Length 19"

Reddish bill, pink feet and light color on wing separates from other Whistling Ducks.

SEXES ALIKE

GEESE

CANADA GOOSE
Branta canadensis

White chin patch on head is exclusive of Canada Goose.

Length 25-43''

SNOW GOOSE
Chen Caerulescens

Black grin patch on bill is exclusive of Snow Goose

Length 25-38''

Length 25-3

SNOW GOOSE
dark phase "Blue"

The "Blue" goose is a color variation of the Lesser Snow Goose species.

64

SEXES ALIKE – ALL GEESE

GEESE

WHITE-FRONTED GOOSE
Anser albifrons

The pinkish bill, white patch on front of head, and dark bars on belly, identify species.

Length 30"

ROSS' GOOSE
Chen rossi

Small pink bill with dark warty base will separate from similar appearing Snow Goose. Bill also lacks the black grin patch.

Length 23"

BRANT
Branta bernicala

Small black bill, whitish markings on neck, and white on rear of body identify the Brant. The Pacific Brant (not shown) is darker.

Length 22-26"

SEXES ALIKE

65

SWANS, CORMORANTS, LOONS

MUTE SWAN
Cygnus olor

Length 60"

WHISTLING SWAN
Olor columbianus
Length 53"

TRUMPETER SWAN
Cygnus buccinator
Length 59"

Summer

Winter

LOON (COMMON)
Gavia immer
Length 31"

DOUBLE-CRESTED CORMORANT
Phalacrocorax auritus
Length 33"

GREBES

HORNED GREBE
Podiceps auritus
Length 13"

Summer   **Winter**

EARED GREBE
Podiceps nigricollis
Length 13"

Summer   **Winter**

PIED-BILLED GREBE
Podilymbus podiceps
Length 13"

Summer   **Winter**

RED-NECKED GREBE
Podiceps grisegena
Length 18"

Summer   **Winter**

WESTERN GREBE
Aechmophorus occidentalis
Length 25"

Summer and Winter

67

FEET

Feet are often a distinguishing characteristic, and are included here so you may check as many features as possible for identification.

Bufflehead male

Green-winged Teal

Ring-necked male

Cinnamon Teal
Blue-winged Teal

Pintail

Redhead
Canvasback

Hooded Merganser

Wood Duck

Wigeon

Bufflehead female
Ring-necked female
Oldsquaw   Ruddy
Lesser and Greater Scaup

Black Scoter

Gadwall

Colors shown are for both sexes except those specifi
Illustrations are for basic color only. Not drawn to sc

FEET

Color variations of Mallard feet

COLOR WILL VARY WITH AGE AND SEASON

Mallard

Goldeneye

Red-breasted & Common Merganser females

White-winged Scoter female

Mallard

Shoveler

Red-breasted & Common Merganser males

Surf Scoter male

Mallard

Surf Scoter female

Black Duck

White-winged Scoter male

Colors shown are for both sexes except those specified.
Illustrations are for basic color only. Not drawn to scale.

FLIGHT LEVELS

MALES

LEVEL 4
LEVEL 3
LEVEL 2
LEVEL 1

Approximate scale

Flight Levels add the extra dimension needed to further identification of ducks at a distance. Most species of birds seem to have a comfort zone – a distance they maintain from possible danger as well as a flying level they adopt during nonmigratory flight. Ducks are no exception and can be observed flying in one of four distinct Levels, depending on species. These Levels are maintained during nonmigratory flight in normal weather conditions over open water, (bad weather conditions will lower the upper flight Levels).

I have depicted the ducks closest together that would be mistaken for each other in flight. Each species will exhibit features that can be studied and compared against the others for identification in flight. Puddle ducks are found in the upper Levels and diving ducks in the lower Levels. Most of the ducks that use Level 1 are not considered palatable for the table.

There will be a greater distance in and between actual flight levels than I was able to show on these pages.

LEVEL 4

1. MALLARD
2. BLACK DUCK
3. GADWALL
4. WIGEON
5. PINTAIL

LEVEL 3

6. NORTHERN SHOVELER
7. CINNAMON TEAL
8. BLUE-WINGED TEAL (FALL)
9. GREEN-WINGED TEAL
10. WOOD DUCK

LEVEL 2

11. COMMON GOLDENEYE
12. LESSER SCAUP
13. GREATER SCAUP
14. RING-NECKED
15. CANVASBACK
16. REDHEAD

LEVEL 1

17. OLDSQUAW
18. BUFFLEHEAD
19. COOT
20. COMMON MERGANSER
21. HOODED MERGANSER
22. RED-BREASTED MERGANSER
23. COMMON EIDER
24. RUDDY
25. BLACK SCOTER
26. SURF SCOTER
27. WHITE-WINGED SCOTER

FLIGHT LEVELS

FEMALES

LEVEL 4
LEVEL 3
LEVEL 2
LEVEL 1

Approximate scale

Most identification books show the males and females together in flight. The viewer is usually quick to identify a species this way, but females are usually recognized only because they are flying in close proximity to the more easily identifiable males. To help further identification, I have separated the females so they can be studied for their own features. Each will exhibit something that will set it apart from the others if studied carefully.

There will be greater distance in and between actual flight levels than I was able to show on these pages.

LEVEL 4

1. BLACK DUCK
2. MALLARD
3. GADWALL
4. WIGEON
5. PINTAIL

LEVEL 3

6. WOOD DUCK
7. NORTHERN SHOVELER
8. CINNAMON TEAL ⎤ IDENTICAL
9. BLUE-WINGED TEAL ⎦
10. GREEN-WINGED TEAL

LEVEL 2

11. COMMON GOLDENEYE
12. LESSER SCAUP
13. GREATER SCAUP
14. REDHEAD
15. RING-NECKED
16. CANVASBACK

LEVEL 1

17. BUFFLEHEAD
18. RUDDY
19. COOT
20. COMMON MERGANSER
21. HOODED MERGANSER
22. RED-BREASTED MERGANSER
23. OLDSQUAW
24. COMMON EIDER
25. BLACK SCOTER
26. SURF SCOTER
27. WHITE-WINGED SCOTER

VERMICULATION

WORM-LIKE OR WAVY LINES ON FEATHERS

First appears on rump or sides of males.

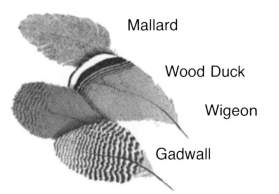

Mallard

Wood Duck

Wigeon

Gadwall

A few of the many types of vermiculation on males.

74

Index

Instructions for Easy Use

Take all measurements of upper bill only — from corner of mouth to tip

1- Place thumbnail at corner of mouth.
2- Line up with base line on pages 2, 3, 4, or 5. (The line connecting bills at bottom).
3- Move along base line until you have closest fit — chart is progressively sized on length.
4- When you have closest size and shape, open to pages indicated.
5- Re-check on the species pages and confirm with other information.
6- If first choice was incorrect — try species each side of original selection.
7- In-flight comparisons are on pages 70-71 and 72-73.
8- Geese, swans, and other waterfowl not shown on charts can be found on pages 58-67.

COLOR WILL VARY WITH AGE AND SEASON — USE CLOSEST SIZE AND SHAPE

SPECIAL NOTE: Female bill sizes are marked by dotted white lines except for those that are similar in size to male. The female bill shapes at top of chart have been reduced and are shown for basic color only. Female bills are shown full size on species pages.